Christmas Ca[rols]
for Vocal Duet

ARRANGED BY DONALD SOSIN

ISBN 978-1-57560-647-7

Visit our website at www.cherrylane.com

CONTENTS

Angels We Have Heard on High

Translated by James Chadwick

Traditional French Carol

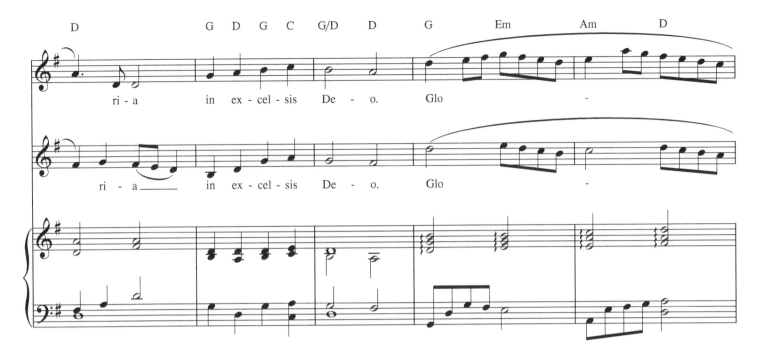

Additional Lyrics

2. Shepherds, why this jubilee?
   Why your joyous strains prolong?
   What the gladsome tidings be
   Which inspire your heavenly song? *(To Chorus)*

3. Come to Bethlehem and see
   Him whose birth the angels sing;
   Come, adore on bended knee,
   Christ the Lord, the newborn King. *(To Chorus)*

4. See Him in a manger laid,
   Whom the choirs of angels praise;
   Mary, Joseph, lend your aid,
   While our hearts in love we raise. *(To Chorus)*

Away in a Manger

Traditional
Words by John T. McFarland (v.3)

Music by James R. Murray

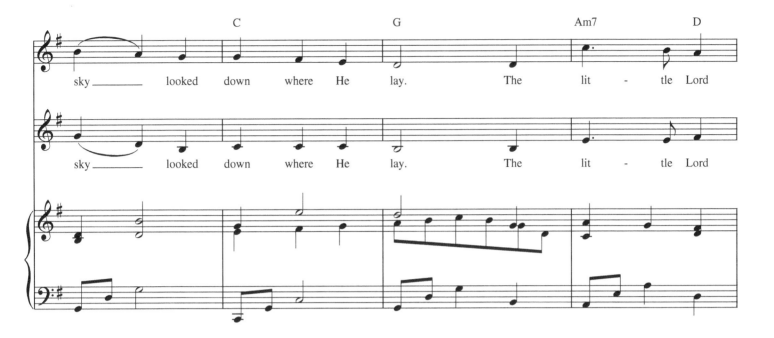

Additional Lyrics

2. The cattle are lowing, the baby awakes,
   But little Lord Jesus no crying He makes.
   I love Thee, Lord Jesus, look down from the sky
   And stay by my cradle 'til morning is nigh.

3. Be near me, Lord Jesus, I ask Thee to stay
   Close by me forever, and love me, I pray.
   Bless all the dear children in Thy tender care,
   And take us to heaven, to live with Thee there.

Deck the Halls

Traditional Welsh Carol

Additional Lyrics

2. See the blazing Yule before us.
   Fa la la la la la la la la.
   Strike the harp and join the chorus.
   Fa la la la la la la la la.
   Follow me in merry measure.
   Fa la la la la la la la la.
   While I tell of Yuletide treasure.
   Fa la la la la la la la la.

3. Fast away the old year passes.
   Fa la la la la la la la.
   Hail the new, ye lads and lasses.
   Fa la la la la la la la.
   Sing we joyous all together.
   Fa la la la la la la la la.
   Heedless of the wind and weather.
   Fa la la la la la la la la.

The First Noel

17th Century English Carol
Music from W. Sandys' *Christmas Carols*

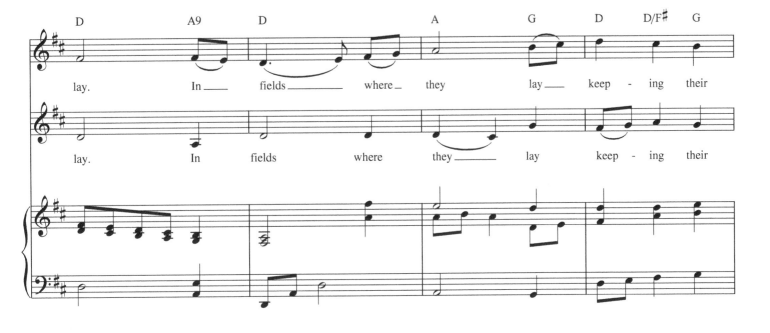

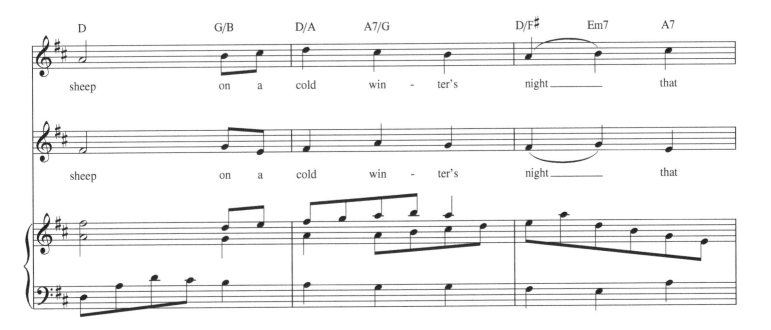

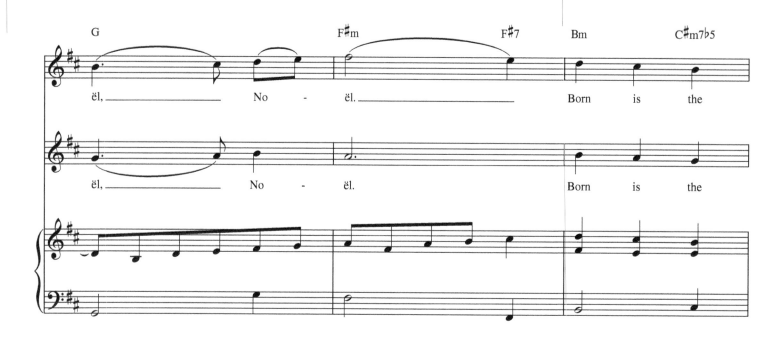

Additional Lyrics

2. They looked up and saw a star
   Shining in the east beyond them far,
   And to the earth it gave great light,
   And so it continued both day and night. *(To Chorus)*

3. And by the light of that same star
   Three wise men came from country far;
   To seek for a king was their intent,
   And to follow the star wherever it went. *(To Chorus)*

Jingle Bells

Words and Music by
J. Pierpont

mak - ing spir - its bright. What fun it is to ride and sing a sleigh - ing song to - night. Oh!

ring, mak - ing spir - its bright. It's fun to ride and sing a sleigh - ing song to - night. Oh!

Chorus

Jin - gle bells, jin - gle bells, jin - gle all the way! Oh, what fun it is to ride in a

Jin - gle bells, jin - gle bells, jin - gle all the way! Oh, what fun it is to ride in a

one - horse o - pen sleigh! Jin - gle bells, jin - gle bells, jin - gle all the way!

one - horse o - pen sleigh! Jin - gle bells, jin - gle bells, jin - gle all the way!

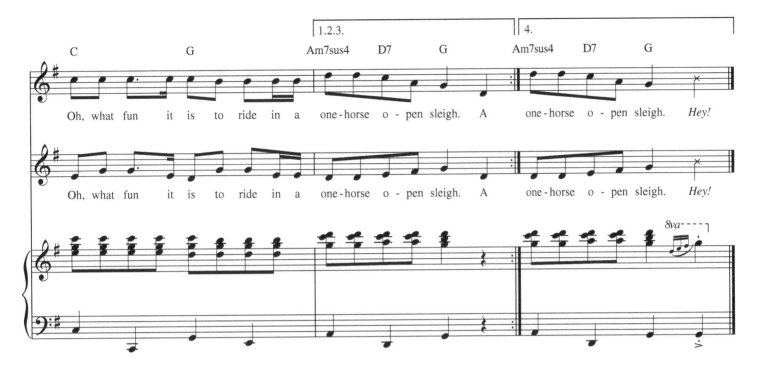

Additional Lyrics

2. A day or two ago,
   I thought I'd take a ride,
   And soon Miss Fanny Bright
   Was seated by my side;
   The horse was lean and lank;
   Misfortune seemed his lot;
   He got into a drifted bank,
   And we, we got upsot. Oh! *(To Chorus)*

3. A day or two ago,
   The story I must tell
   I went out on the snow
   And on my back I fell;
   A gent was riding by
   In a one-horse open sleigh,
   He laughed as there I sprawling lie,
   But quickly drove away. Oh! *(To Chorus)*

4. Now the ground is white
   Go it while you're young,
   Take the girls tonight
   And sing this sleighing song;
   Just get a bob-tailed bay,
   Two forty as his speed
   Hitch him to an open sleigh
   And crack! you'll take the lead. Oh! *(To Chorus)*

God Rest Ye Merry, Gentlemen

19th Century English Carol

Additional Lyrics

2. From God our heavenly Father
   A blessed angel came;
   And unto certain shepherds
   Brought tidings of the same;
   How that in Bethlehem was born
   The Son of God by name.
   O tidings, *etc.*

3. "Fear not, then," said the angel,
   "Let nothing you affright;
   This day is born a Saviour
   Of a pure virgin bright,
   To free all those who trust in him
   From Satan's power and might."
   O tidings, *etc.*

4. Now to the Lord sing praises,
   All you within this place,
   And with true love and brotherhood
   Each other now embrace;
   This holy tide of Christmas
   Doth bring redeeming grace.
   O tidings, *etc.*

Hark! The Herald Angels Sing

Words by Charles Wesley
Altered by George Whitefield

Music by Felix Mendelssohn-Bartholdy
Arranged by William H. Cummings

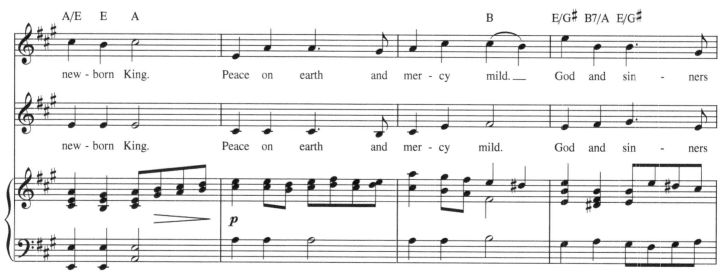

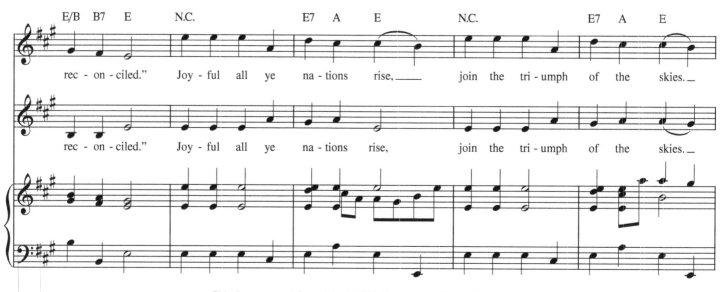

Additional Lyrics

2. Christ, by highest heav'n adored:
   Christ, the everlasting Lord;
   Late in time behold him come,
   Offspring of the favored one.
   Veil'd in flesh, the Godhead see;
   Hail, th'incarnate Deity:
   Pleased, as man, with men to dwell,
   Jesus, our Emmanuel!
   Hark! the herald angels sing,
   "Glory to the newborn King!"

3. Hail! the heav'n-born Prince of peace!
   Hail! the Son of Righteousness!
   Light and life to all he brings,
   Risen with healing in his wings
   Mild he lays his glory by,
   Born that man no more may die:
   Born to raise the son of earth,
   Born to give them second birth.
   Hark! the herald angels sing,
   "Glory to the newborn King!"

It Came Upon the Midnight Clear

Words by Edmund Hamilton Sears

Music by Richard Storrs Willis

Additional Lyrics

2. Yet with the woes of sin and strife
   The world has suffered long,
   Beneath the angel strain have rolled
   Two thousand years of wrong;
   And man, at war with man, hears not
   The love song which they bring:
   O hush the noise, ye men of strife,
   And hear the angels sing!

3. Still through the cloven skies they come,
   With peaceful wings unfurl'd;
   And still their heav'nly music floats
   O'er all the weary world:
   Above its sad and lowly plains
   They bend on hov'ring wing,
   And ever o'er its Babel sounds
   The blessed angels sing.

4. All ye, beneath life's crushing load,
   Whose forms are bending low,
   Who toil along the climbing way
   With painful steps and slow,
   Look, now! for glad and golden hours
   Come swiftly on the wing:
   O rest beside the weary road,
   And hear the angels sing!

Joy to the World

Words by Isaac Watts

Music by George Frideric Handel
Arranged by Lowell Mason

Additional Lyrics

2. Joy to the world! The Savior reigns
   Let men their songs employ.
   While fields and floods, rocks, hills, and plains
   Repeat the sounding joy,
   Repeat the sounding joy,
   Repeat the sounding joy.

3. He rules the world with truth and grace,
   And makes the nations prove
   The glories of His righteousness.
   And wonders of His love,
   And wonders of His love,
   And wonders, wonders of His love.

O Christmas Tree
(O Tannenbaum)

Traditional German Carol

Additional Lyrics

2. O Christmas tree, O Christmas tree,
   Much pleasure doth thou bring me!
   O Christmas tree, O Christmas tree,
   Much pleasure doth thou bring me!
   For every year the Christmas tree
   Brings to us all both joy and glee.
   O Christmas tree, O Christmas tree,
   Much pleasure doth thou bring me!

3. O Christmas tree, O Christmas tree,
   Thy candles shine out brightly!
   O Christmas tree, O Christmas tree,
   Thy candles shine out brightly!
   Each bough doth hold its tiny light
   That makes each toy to sparkle bright.
   O Christmas tree, O Christmas tree,
   Thy candles shine out brightly!

4. O Christmas tree, O Christmas tree!
   Thou has a wondrous message:
   O Christmas tree, O Christmas tree!
   Thou has a wondrous message:
   Thou dost proclaim the Savior's birth;
   Good will to men and peace on earth.
   O Christmas tree, O Christmas tree!
   Thou has a wondrous message.

O Come, All Ye Faithful

(Adeste Fideles)

Words and Music by John Francis Wade
Latin Words translated by Frederick Oakeley

Additional Lyrics

2. Sing, choirs of angels, sing in exultation;
   Sing, all ye citizens of heaven above!
   Glory to God, all glory in the highest.
   O Come, let us adore Him, *etc.*

3. See how the shepherds, summoned to His cradle,
   Leaving their flocks, draw nigh to gaze;
   We too will thither bend our joyful footsteps.
   O Come, let us adore Him, *etc.*

4. Yea, Lord, we greet Thee, born this happy morning;
   Jesus, to Thee be glory given;
   Word of the Father, now in flesh appearing.
   O Come, let us adore Him, *etc.*

O Holy Night

French Words by Placide Cappeau
English Words by John S. Dwight

Music by Adolphe Adam

Moderately, flowingly

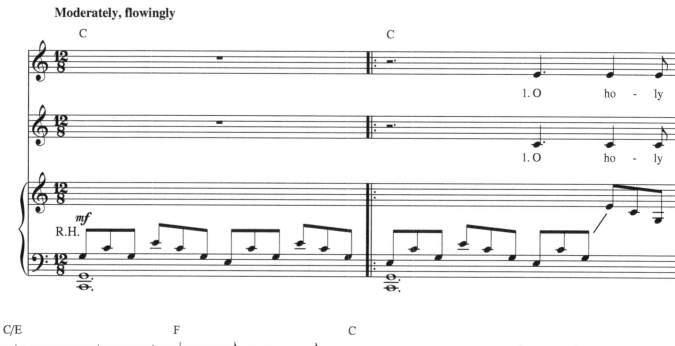

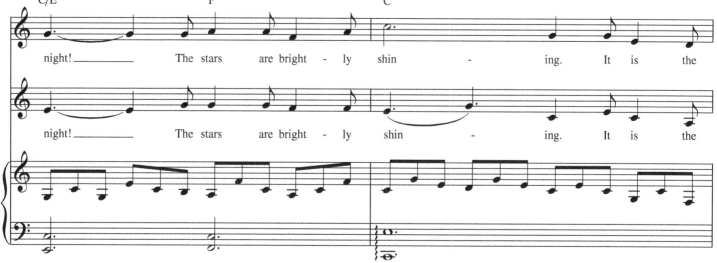

world _____ in sin and er - ror pin - ing till He ap - peared and the soul felt its

world _____ in sin and er - ror pin - ing till He ap - peared and the soul felt its

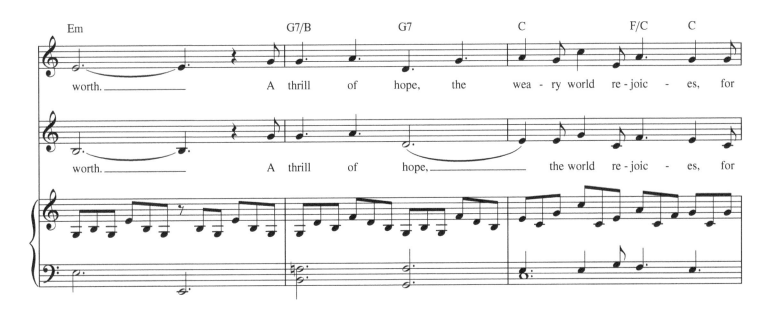

worth. _____ A thrill of hope, the wea - ry world re - joic - es, for

worth. _____ A thrill of hope, _____ the world re - joic - es, for

yon - der breaks a new and glo - rious morn.

yon - der breaks a new and glo - rious morn.

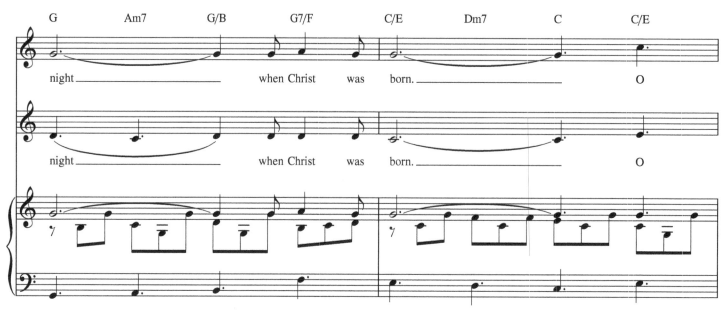

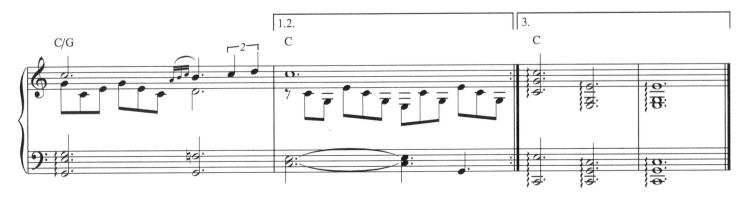

Additional Lyrics

2. Led by the light of Faith serenely beaming
   With glowing hearts by His cradle we stand.
   So led by light of a star sweetly gleaming
   Here come the wise men from Orient land.
   The King of Kings lay thus in lowly manger
   In all our trials born to be our friend.
   Fall on your knees, etc.

3. Truly He taught us to love one another;
   His law is love and His gospel is peace.
   Chains shall He break, for the slave is our brother,
   And in His name all oppression shall cease.
   Sweet hymns of joy in grateful chorus raise we.
   Let all within us praise His holy name.
   Fall on your knees, *etc.*

O Little Town of Bethlehem

Words by Phillips Brooks

Music by Lewis H. Redner

1. O lit- tle town of Beth- le- hem, how still we __ see thee

lie. A- bove thy deep and dream- less sleep the si- lent __ stars go

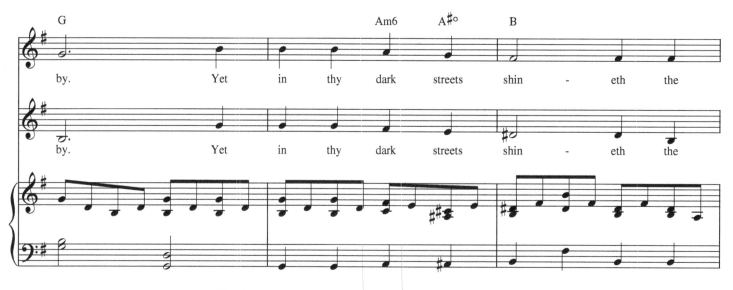

by. Yet in thy dark streets shin- eth the

Additional Lyrics

2. For Christ is born of Mary,
   And gathered all above
   While mortals sleep, the angels keep
   Their watch of wondering love.
   O morning stars, together
   Proclaim the holy birth,
   And praises sing to God the king,
   And peace to all the earth!

3. How silently, how silently
   The wondrous gift is given!
   So God imparts to human hearts
   The blessings of his heaven.
   No ear may hear his coming;
   But in this world of sin,
   Where meek souls will receive him, still
   The dear Christ enters in.

Silent Night

Words by Joseph Mohr
Translated by John F. Young

Music by Franz X. Gruber

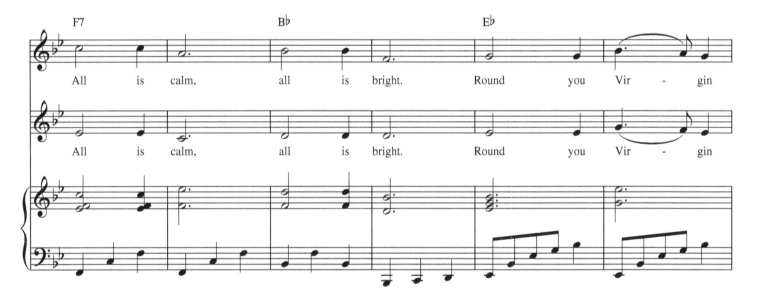

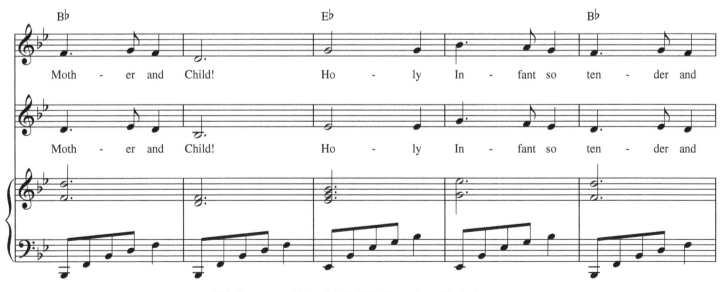

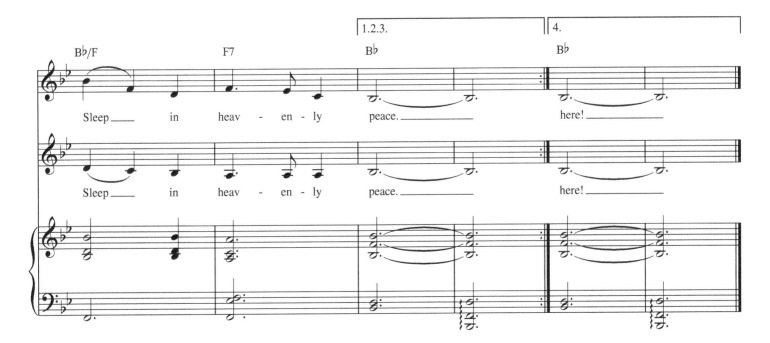

Additional Lyrics

2. Silent night, Holy night.
   Shepherds quake at the sight.
   Glories stream from heav'n afar;
   Heavenly hosts sing Alleluia.
   Christ the Savior is born.
   Christ the Savior is born.

3. Silent Night, Holy Night.
   Son of God, love's pure light.
   Radiant beams from Thy Holy Face.
   With the dawn of redeeming grace.
   Jesus, Lord, at Thy birth.
   Jesus, Lord, at Thy birth.

4. Silent night, holy night,
   Wondrous star, lend thy light
   With the angels let us sing
   Alleluia to our King
   Christ the Savior is here,
   Jesus the Savior is here!

The Twelve Days of Christmas

Traditional English Carol

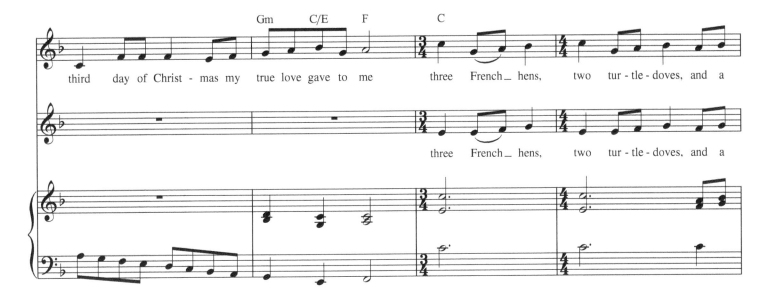

*Substitute "sixth," "seventh," "eighth," etc., for each successive verse.
**Skip to appropriate number. For 12th day, continue without skipping.

We Three Kings of Orient Are

Words and Music by
John H. Hopkins, Jr.

Additional Lyrics

2. Born a King on Bethlehem's plain,
   Gold we bring to crown Him again,
   King forever, ceasing never,
   Over us all to reign.
   O, star of wonder, *etc.*

3. Frankincense to offer have I;
   Incense owns a Deity nigh.
   Prayer and praising voices raising,
   Worshiping God on high.
   O, star of wonder, *etc.*

4. Myrrh is mine; its bitter perfume
   Breathes a life of gathering gloom.
   Sorrowing, sighing, bleeding, dying,
   Sealed in the stone-cold tomb.
   O, star of wonder, *etc.*

We Wish You a Merry Christmas

Traditional English Folksong

Additional Lyrics

2. We all love figgy pudding,
    We all love figgy pudding,
    We all love figgy pudding,
    So bring some out here!

3. We won't go until we get some,
    We won't go until we get some,
    We won't go until we get some,
    So bring some out here!

What Child Is This?

Words by William C. Dix

16th Century English Melody

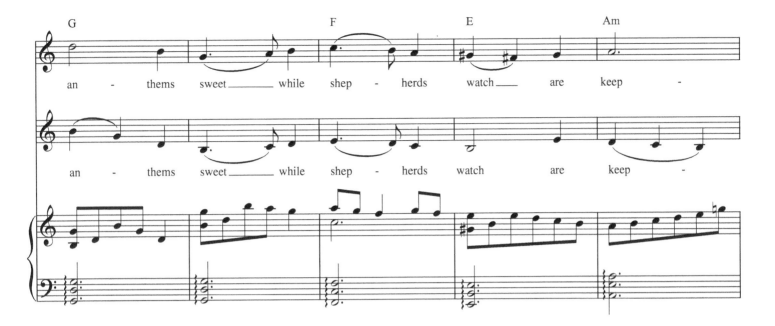

an - thems sweet _____ while shep - herds watch _____ are keep -

an - thems sweet _____ while shep - herds watch are keep -

ing? This, this _____ is Christ the King _____ whom

ing? This, this _____ is Christ the King _____ whom

shep - herds guard _____ and an - gels sing. Haste,

shep - herds guard _____ and an - gels sing. _____ Haste,

haste _____ to bring Him laud, _____ the Babe, _____ the

haste _____ to bring Him laud, _____ the Babe, _____ the

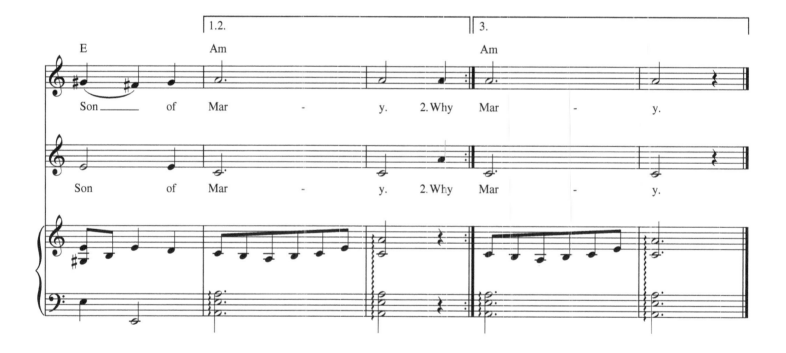

Son _____ of Mar - y. 2. Why Mar - y.

Son of Mar - y. 2. Why Mar - y.

Additional Lyrics

2. Why lies He in such mean estate,
   Where ox and ass are feeding?
   Good Christians, fear, for sinners here
   The silent Word is pleading.
   Nails, spear shall pierce Him through,
   The cross be borne for me, for you.
   Hail, hail the Word made flesh,
   The Babe, the Son of Mary.

3. So bring Him incense, gold and myrrh,
   Come peasant, king to own Him;
   The King of kings salvation brings,
   Let loving hearts enthrone Him.
   Raise, raise a song on high,
   The virgin sings her lullaby.
   Joy, joy for Christ is born,
   The Babe, the Son of Mary.

CHRISTMAS COLLECTIONS
FROM HAL LEONARD
ALL BOOKS ARRANGED FOR PIANO, VOICE & GUITAR

THE BEST CHRISTMAS SONGS EVER

69 all-time favorites: Auld Lang Syne • Coventry Carol • Frosty the Snow Man • Happy Holiday • It Came Upon the Midnight Clear • O Holy Night • Rudolph the Red-Nosed Reindeer • Silver Bells • What Child Is This? • and many more.
00359130 ....$29.99

THE BIG BOOK OF CHRISTMAS SONGS

Over 120 all-time favorites and hard-to-find classics: As Each Happy Christmas • The Boar's Head Carol • Carol of the Bells • Deck the Halls • The Friendly Beasts • God Rest Ye Merry Gentlemen • Joy to the World • Masters in This Hall • O Holy Night • Story of the Shepherd • and more.
00311520 ....$22.99

CHRISTMAS SONGS – BUDGET BOOKS

100 holiday favorites: All I Want for Christmas Is You • Christmas Time Is Here • Feliz Navidad • Grandma Got Run Over by a Reindeer • I'll Be Home for Christmas • Last Christmas • O Holy Night • Please Come Home for Christmas • Rockin' Around the Christmas Tree • We Need a Little Christmas • What Child Is This? • and more.
00310887 ....$15.99

CHRISTMAS MOVIE SONGS

34 holiday hits from the big screen: All I Want for Christmas Is You • Believe • Christmas Vacation • Do You Want to Build a Snowman? • Frosty the Snow Man • Have Yourself a Merry Little Christmas • It's Beginning to Look like Christmas • Mele Kalikimaka • Rudolph the Red-Nosed Reindeer • Silver Bells • White Christmas • You're a Mean One, Mr. Grinch • and more.
00146961 ....$19.99

CHRISTMAS PIANO SONGS FOR DUMMIES®

56 favorites: Auld Lang Syne • Away in a Manger • Blue Christmas • The Christmas Song • Deck the Hall • I'll Be Home for Christmas • Jingle Bells • Joy to the World • My Favorite Things • Silent Night • more!
00311387 ....$19.95

CHRISTMAS POP STANDARDS

22 contemporary holiday hits, including: All I Want for Christmas Is You • Christmas Time Is Here • Little Saint Nick • Mary, Did You Know? • Merry Christmas, Darling • Santa Baby • Underneath the Tree • Where Are You Christmas? • and more.
00348998 ....$14.99

CHRISTMAS SING-ALONG

40 seasonal favorites: Away in a Manger • Christmas Time Is Here • Feliz Navidad • Happy Holiday • Jingle Bells • Mary, Did You Know? • O Come, All Ye Faithful • Rudolph the Red-Nosed Reindeer • Silent Night • White Christmas • and more. Includes online sing-along backing tracks.
00278176 Book/Online Audio $24.99

100 CHRISTMAS CAROLS

Includes: Away in a Manger • Bring a Torch, Jeannette, Isabella • Coventry Carol • Deck the Hall • The First Noel • Go, Tell It on the Mountain • I Heard the Bells on Christmas Day • Joy to the World • O Come, All Ye Faithful (Adeste Fideles) • Silent Night • Sing We Now of Christmas • and more.
00310897 ....$19.99

100 MOST BEAUTIFUL CHRISTMAS SONGS

Includes: Angels We Have Heard on High • Baby, It's Cold Outside • Christmas Time Is Here • Do You Hear What I Hear • Grown-Up Christmas List • Happy Xmas (War Is Over) • I'll Be Home for Christmas • The Little Drummer Boy • Mary, Did You Know? • O Holy Night • White Christmas • Winter Wonderland • and more.
00237285 ....$29.99

POPULAR CHRISTMAS SHEET MUSIC: 1980-2017

40 recent seasonal favorites: All I Want for Christmas Is You • Because It's Christmas (For All the Children) • Breath of Heaven (Mary's Song) • Christmas Lights • The Christmas Shoes • The Gift • Grown-Up Christmas List • Last Christmas • Santa Tell Me • Snowman • Where Are You Christmas? • Wrapped in Red • and more.
00278089 ....$22.99

A SENTIMENTAL CHRISTMAS BOOK

27 beloved Christmas favorites, including: The Christmas Shoes • The Christmas Song (Chestnuts Roasting on an Open Fire) • Christmas Time Is Here • Grown-Up Christmas List • Have Yourself a Merry Little Christmas • I'll Be Home for Christmas • Somewhere in My Memory • Where Are You Christmas? • and more.
00236830 ....$14.99

ULTIMATE CHRISTMAS

100 seasonal favorites: Auld Lang Syne • Bring a Torch, Jeannette, Isabella • Carol of the Bells • The Chipmunk Song • Christmas Time Is Here • The First Noel • Frosty the Snow Man • Gesù Bambino • Happy Holiday • Happy Xmas (War Is Over) • Jingle-Bell Rock • Pretty Paper • Silver Bells • Suzy Snowflake • and more.
00361399 ....$24.99

A VERY MERRY CHRISTMAS

39 familiar favorites: Blue Christmas • Feliz Navidad • Happy Xmas (War Is Over) • I'll Be Home for Christmas • Jingle-Bell Rock • Please Come Home for Christmas • Rockin' Around the Christmas Tree • Santa, Bring My Baby Back (To Me) • Sleigh Ride • White Christmas • and more.
00310536 ....$14.99

HAL•LEONARD®

Complete contents listings available online at www.halleonard.com

PRICES, CONTENTS, AND AVAILABILITY SUBJECT TO CHANGE WITHOUT NOTICE.

MUSIC BUSINESS MUST-HAVES

ALL YOU NEED TO KNOW ABOUT THE MUSIC BUSINESS – 8TH EDITION

by Donald S. Passman
Free Press

The definitive and essential guide to the music industry, now in its eighth edition – revised and updated with crucial information on the industry's major changes in response to rapid technological advances and economic uncertainty.

00119121 ....$32.00

ENGAGING THE CONCERT AUDIENCE

by David Wallace
Berklee Press

Learn to engage, excite, captivate and expand your audience! These practical techniques will help you to communicate with your listeners on a deeper, more interactive level.
As you do, the concert experience will become more meaningful, and the bond between you and your audience will grow.

00244532 Book/Online Media $16.99

HOW TO GET A JOB IN THE MUSIC INDUSTRY – 3RD EDITION

by Keith Hatschek with Breanne Beseda
Berklee Press

This third edition includes a new career tool kit and social media strategy. Inside you'll find: details on booming job prospects in digital music distribution and music licensing; interviews with nine music industry professionals under 35 who discuss how they got their starts, plus what skills today's leading job candidates must possess; and much more.

00130699 ....$27.99

MANAGING YOUR BAND – SIXTH EDITION

Artist Management:
The Ultimate Responsibility

by Stephen Marcone with David Philp

From dive bars to festivals, from branding and merchandising to marketing and publicity, from publishing and licensing to rights and contracts, Marcone and Philp leave no stone unturned in this comprehensive guide to artist management.

00200476 ....$34.95

MELODY IN SONGWRITING

by Jack Perricone
Berklee Press

Discover songwriting techniques from the hit makers!
This comprehensive guide unlocks the secrets of hit songs, examining them, and revealing why they succeed. Learn to write memorable melodies and discover the dynamic relationships between melody, harmony, rhythm, and rhyme.

50449419 ....$26.99

MUSIC LAW IN THE DIGITAL AGE – 2ND EDITION

by Allen Bargfrede
Berklee Press

With the free-form exchange of music files and musical ideas online, understanding copyright laws has become essential to career success in the new music marketplace. This cutting-edge, plain-language guide shows you how copyright law drives the contemporary music industry.

00148196 ....$22.99

MUSIC MARKETING

by Mike King
Berklee Press

Sell more music! Learn the most effective marketing strategies available to musicians, leveraging the important changes and opportunities that the digital age has brought to music marketing. This multifaceted and integrated approach will help you to develop an effective worldwide marketing strategy.

50449588 ....$24.99

PAT PATTISON'S SONGWRITING: ESSENTIAL GUIDE TO RHYMING – 2ND EDITION

Berklee Press

If you have written lyrics before, even at a professional level, you can still gain greater control and understanding of your craft with the exercises and worksheets included in this book. Hone your writing technique and skill with this practical and fun approach to the art of lyric writing.

00124366 ....$22.98

THE PLAIN AND SIMPLE GUIDE TO MUSIC PUBLISHING – 4TH EDITION

by Randall D. Wixen

In this expanded and updated third edition, Randall D. Wixen adds greater depth to such increasingly important topics as the rapidly shifting industry paradigms, the growing importance of streaming and subscription models, a discussion of new compulsary license media, and so much more.

00301384 ....$24.99

PROJECT MANAGEMENT FOR MUSICIANS

by Jonathan Feist
Berklee Press

Get organized, and take charge of your music projects! You will learn to: develop work strategies; delegate tasks; build and manage teams; organize your project office; develop production schedules; understand and organize contracts; analyze risk; and much more.

50449659 ....$39.99

SONGWRITING: ESSENTIAL GUIDE TO LYRIC FORM AND STRUCTURE

by Pat Pattison
Berklee Press

Veteran songwriter Pat Pattison has taught many of Berklee College of Music's best and brightest students how to write truly great lyrics. Her helpful guide contains essential information on lyric structures, timing and placement, and exercises to help everyone from beginners to seasoned songwriters say things more effectively and gain a better understanding of their craft.

50481582 ....$19.99

SONGWRITING STRATEGIES

by Mark Simos
Berklee Press

Write songs starting from any direction: melody, lyric, harmony, rhythm, or idea. This book will help you expand your range and flexibility as a songwriter. Discussions, hands-on exercises, and notated examples will help you hone your craft. This creatively liberating approach supports the overall integrity of emotion and meaning in your songs.

50449621 ....$24.99

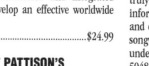

HAL•LEONARD®

www.halleonard.com

Prices, content, and availability subject to change without notice.

0922
190